the age of reasons

the Age of reasons

UNCOLLECTED POEMS

1969–1982

EDITED BY MILES CHAMPION

TED GREENWALD

WESLEYAN UNIVERSITY PRESS

MIDDLETOWN, CONNECTICUT

Wesleyan University Press

Middletown CT 06459

www.wesleyan.edu/wespress

2016 © Ted Greenwald

Editor's Note © 2016 by Miles Champion

Manufactured in the United States of America

Designed and Typeset in Parkinson Electra Pro

by Eric M. Brooks

ART WORKS.
arts.gov

*This project is supported in part by an award from
the National Endowment for the Arts.*

Library of Congress
Cataloging-in-Publication Data
Greenwald, Ted.
[Poems. Selections]
The age of reasons: uncollected poems 1969–1982 /
Ted Greenwald; edited by Miles Champion.
    pages; cm
ISBN 978-0-8195-7626-2 (pbk.) —
ISBN 978-0-8195-7627-9 (ebook)
I. Champion, Miles, 1968– II. Title.
PS3557.R3968A6   2016
811'.54 — dc23   2015031902

5 4 3 2 1

TO KIT

CONTENTS

EDITOR'S NOTE

Ted Greenwald has written on a daily basis for more than fifty years. So prolific has he been, in fact, that the poems in *The Age of Reasons* are selected from more than two hundred uncollected poems Greenwald published in magazines between 1969 and 1982, years in which he published sixteen books. In some ways, then, the present volume can be regarded as a companion to *Common Sense*, a selection of Greenwald's early poems edited by Curtis Faville and published by his L Publications imprint in 1978. Happily, Wesleyan University Press is reissuing *Common Sense* to coincide with the publication of *The Age of Reasons.*

Like many important poets, Greenwald cannot be pigeonholed as belonging to any particular literary movement, and his work evades easy categorization. A formalist with an unrivaled ear for everyday speech, we might situate him as running productive interference between his contemporaries in the second generation of the New York School, and the Language poets, for whom he is a foundational figure. His poetry is of the everyday and the ordinary, but rid of the cocktail-hour urbanity that sometimes mars the more uptown products of the New York School. Its relevance for Language poetry lies primarily in the fact that Greenwald often lets the form or sound of his poems guide them, rather than their sense.

The Age of Reasons presents a wider range of Greenwald's forms and approaches than is usual in his books. We encounter Greenwald the minimalist, but while it is tempting to point to Aram Saroyan and Robert Grenier as fellow travelers, Greenwald's aesthetic is different, his palette emphatically more vernacular. His minimalist works, here, are offset by extended pieces composed of verse paragraphs, in which we find Greenwald at his most conceptual (inasmuch as the works function "almost like plans for the future").[1] If there is another organizing motif as disarmingly simple and casually brilliant as "The Sandwich Islands," in which every paragraph is both a sandwich and an island, I have yet to encounter it. Indeed, Charles Bernstein has posited the casual made strange—speech unhinged from utility—as the central "Greenwaldian paradox."[2] Whatever the scale, the light in Greenwald's poems is always natural, the surface flat and cool. There are no deep images, although Greenwald understands as intuitively as Ted Berrigan that the surface is more interestingly located at some depth.

Also included in this selection is Greenwald's play, *The Coast*, which infuses Beckettian waiting with a sensibility borrowed from art-world happenings.[3] Greenwald was involved in that world, of course, having curated readings at Holly Solomon's 98 Greene Street loft, the Clocktower, and MoMA PS1, and collaborated with artist friends Richard Bosman, Les Levine, Gordon Matta-Clark, and George Schneeman.

Prior to assembling this book, my intention was to present uncollected poems from the first twenty years of Greenwald's writing, from 1962 to 1982. I settled on the narrower frame partly because the best of Greenwald's early poems are included in *Common Sense*[4] and partly because the 1969 start date finds Greenwald already writing what are immediately recognizable as "Ted Greenwald poems." Of the poems collected here, "Heartstrings" perhaps gestures most straightforwardly toward what Bill Berkson has termed the "bright abstract scatter" of Greenwald's early work.[5] But Greenwald *becomes* Greenwald, we might argue, when he dispenses with the fragmented forms and collage techniques so often associated with modernism—the problem with them being, in his view, that "there is no everyday language that can be used to test goodness of fit."[6] His poetry, in turn, becomes a thought process: writing as thinking on the page.

Not included here, although the time frames overlap, are works that explore the mutated triolet form ABCA CDAB, which was to increasingly occupy Greenwald from the late seventies through the eighties and beyond. It is for these works that he is best known, works that recharge what's in the air even as they archive American ordinary language.[7] A good number of these frequently book-length poems are available elsewhere, and in *The Age of Reasons* I was keen to present lesser-known aspects of Greenwald's work.

It has been my pleasure to gather these poems over twenty years of friendship with Ted; I thank him for writing them, and for allowing me to arrange them as I saw fit. My thanks also to David Ball, Barbara Barg, Bill Berkson, Charles Bernstein, Steve Clay, Dennis Cooper, Peter Gizzi, Ralph Hawkins, Rob Holloway, Patricia Spears Jones, Gary Lenhart, Greg Masters, Joan McClusky, Maureen Owen, Ron Padgett, Arlo Quint, Tom Raworth, Kit Robinson, Katie Schneeman, Stacy Szymaszek, Fred Wah, and Bill Zavatsky for their help, and to ace Poetry Project interns Sara Akant and Ace McNamara. Ted and I would both like to thank Suzanna Tamminen and her staff at Wesleyan University Press for their care, and the late George Schneeman for his great cover image.

Thanks are also due the editors and publishers of the journals, magazines, and newspapers in which these works first appeared: *#*, *A Hundred Posters*, *Adventures in Poetry*, *African Golfer*, *Big Deal*, *The Big House* (Ailanthus Press), *Blue Pig*, *The Human Handkerchief*, *Là-bas*, *Mag City*, *New York Times*, *Oculist Witnesses*, *Out There*, *The Paris Review*, *Partisan Review/3*, *Rocky Ledge*, *Roof*, *Salome*, *Shell*, *Shirt*, *Straits*, *Tangerine*, *Telephone*, *the*, *This*, *Un Poco Loco*, *United Artists*, *W.B.*, *washington review of the arts*, and *The World*.

MC, January 2016

NOTES

1. Ted Greenwald, "Spoken," *L=A=N=G=U=A=G=E*, vol. 2, no. 7 (March 1979): n.p. See also the four prose works "No Eating," "No Doubt," "No Way," and "No Regrets," recently collected in *Own Church* (Spuyten Duyvil, 2016).

2. Charles Bernstein, unpublished essay on Greenwald's work, shared with the editor on March 26, 2015.

3. *The Coast* was performed at 541 Broadway over three nights in October

1978, with a cast of Tom Carey, Bob Holman, Eileen Myles, and Bob Rosenthal, and costumes by Judith Shea.

4. See "And, Hinges," "I Hear a Step," "Lapstrake," "Pore Suspension," "Privets Come into Season at High Tide," and "Wash" (all 1964); as well as "Bleep" and "Elegance and Umbrellas" (both 1967). See also *Licorice Chronicles*, written between 1964 and 1969 and published by the Kulchur Foundation in 1979.

5. Bill Berkson, "In Ted Greenwald," *L=A=N=G=U=A=G=E*, vol. 2, no. 7 (March 1979): n.p.

6. Greenwald, "Spoken."

7. For an early, and discrete, example, see "Finally Understanding" in "Language Sampler," ed. Charles Bernstein, *The Paris Review* 86 (Winter 1982): n.p. See also *Exit the Face* (with Richard Bosman; The Museum of Modern Art, New York, 1982) and "Going into School That Day" in 3 (Cuneiform Press, 2008), among many others.

the age of reasons

man
who write
one
million poems
in
one
day
maybe
know what's up

I light
cigaret
rain smoke

SHOW AND TELL

When I first saw you
I liked you   You
didn't come on the way
you thought you came on
My first impression of you was
you're a person
who I'm really glad to know
who's interested
in intellectual thoughts and true meanings of things
and I figured
since I was so glad to really get to know you
you'd be pretty glad to get to know me
and maybe I would touch your face with my hands
like I'm in the process of doing now
and look at you at arm's distance
and then closer in
when and if it's ok with you
and we could walk out of this room
arm-in-arm or shoulder-to-shoulder
just touching every other step or so
and go get a coke
or a pepsi and some grilled cheese
I really'd like a cheeseburger more
and talk about books and movies
and just exchange
if you'd want to do that with me
intellectual thoughts
and true meanings   Just
about ourselves   We would be able
to share and explore

all the little thoughts and feelings
that really can mess up the day
if things don't go right
and all the quote irritations of modern living unquote
that Chekhov discussed so well
and then maybe we could learn to be friends
in this process of discovering
what makes each other tick
Pass me a cigaret
and pass me a cup of coffee   Maybe
if we learn to really like one another
I'll sit next to you the next session we have
and Bob and John and Alice and Kit
and you and me
will move our chairs a lot closer together
and really begin to understand
what really makes us tick in the mind
and straighten out our true meanings
We'll call each other on the phone
write letters and postcards to each other
when we're away for vacation
and write poems about what we do each day
and really all the love
even while a lot of loneliness exists in the world
and how we learn each other's quirks
We'll better cope with anything *and anyone*
that might come up and we might meet
and we'll rent a farm
and start a commune
that probably won't be as easy as starting a car

and we'll skinny dip in the pond
take planes to Europe
help the disadvantaged and underdeveloped
make the world a better place to grow in
and when we get old
we'll look back *on all this*
and know just know
just six of us had the power
to change the course of things
by learning to get along better
and it all started
with us sitting down
looking each other straight in the eye
and rapping

air like art
moves
from
the
window
eyes look out
waves of light
spin webs in limbs
a sunny side of the street gives shadows hats
exclamation
point
a yellow sweater folds

POEM

at this point in history
tremulous sweeps can be heard
by the now-defunct brooms
that have just this second become necessary
to the oncoming madness of the self
the self and its other
sets up conditions
a) as I said
b) as I take
c) as I get
music is in the makeup
at any minute arousing thoughts of flowers,
or lips   that shape notes in conjunction
(like stars) with the tongue
the language times use to talk through the petals
so sweet the head shakes
the other meantimes, on a particular evening,
stares rocking in disbelief
not seeing the we for what it is without clothes
the he and she
leaving the door open to memories of nature
dynamite carried by swans

A GOOD NIGHT'S

a good night's
sleep does wonders
for the disposition
disposes of sleep
supposes a desire
to wind up
and pitch curves
through a brain
curling like a
spring through landscape
a dream, like
a plane high
up complains to
a chair in
a hotel lobby
a convention enters
town and sweeps
past the speakers
in a gown
the speakers go
to supper, talk
awhile, go up
and go to
sleep amidst whooping
shrubs and small
comprehension-size animals
protectively colorated so
they don't wake

if a toenail
like the halfmoon
hits the Hudson
of the window

do
they
worry
no
but
the
brain
is
a
funny
thing

WAITING SPOON

A round room

The flowers are in bloom

Sun blossoms the window

A low sound

The boom

Ray gun down

A found objection

The friend in a comb

Kills some in the town

A bone

AIR

tongue no spit tonight out
whistling between nerves
the peels urge governing bodies
without or from within

counting luckiness
the old gun back of my head
tasting of definiteness

hanging out and hanging around

seeing and being seen

going to sleep and waking

comings and goings

hello loneliness hello happiness hello
sweet caress I think I'm going to die

I LOVE YOU

I love you
So much
I'm beside myself
That's the other me
Beside me
Passing into dust
Against the side
Of the beautiful girl
Coming to decide
I'm a beautiful woman
And maybe
I like myself I don't
Like myself
Besides us
Passing into dust
Against the side
Of the we
We're separated into
Something breezelike
Without guarantees
But whatever you are
That I feel home
And no getting away
From it or with anything
Without you
Everything's everything
And me

(I can't really
Speak for you)
Nothing in particular
No place, neither

SOMEBODY WANTS YOU

mental institutions that make it take it
easy
dressers with drawers with goals
in mind
custody built (nor those a) a shanty

behavior wrong by objective test

a desire to learn geography

a desire to plunge anywhere

particularly the personal worlds of congestion

in the ward together
for drama for conversational
play much part
has been
to or is a

shoulder to shoulder to face
the public
breasting these civilities

friendliness

you find in lobbies
intimate against undue
slowed down your movements
or accidents

on the strength of

shifts in posture
directly across from you, and so forth

and so forth

THE COAST

Guard 1: What time's it?

Guard 2: Don't know. Left my watch home.

Guard 1: What's that on your arm?

Guard 2: Bracelet. (Lights cigaret, offers one to Guard 1)

Guard 1: No thanks. (Takes out a box) Want a cough drop?

Guard 2: No. Thanks anyway. Anyone tell you how come we can't cough?

Guard 1: Secret. It's okay with me, though. I haven't had a cough in almost a year.

Guard 2: Me neither. Makes me kind of curious though. Figured, why take chances and bought a box of cough drops on the way over.

Guard 1: The money's good, so who's going to complain.

Guard 2: Not me, for sure.

Guard 1: Me neither.

(They walk around a little   Both wear crepe shoes   Flashlights hither and yon   Walk back)

Guard 1: Nothing.

Guard 2: Been that way more than a month now.

Guard 1: Sure wish something would happen. Can't go on eating cough drops all night.

(Third Guard walks up)

Guard 3: Everything quiet?

Guard 2: Not a peep. Nothing.

Guard 1: Nothing. Everything quiet where you been?

Guard 3: Not a sound. Been on this job more than a year, not a sound. Haven't missed a night either.

(Fourth Guard walks in)

Guard 4: Hear anything?

Guard 3: Nothing.

Guard 4: Been doing this two years and not a peep. Two years now. Good job, though. Nice and quiet.

Guard 1: Sort of gets to you a little.

Guard 4: Just in the beginning. You get used to it.

Guard 1: I'm sure it'll go away. I'm not worried about that.

Guard 3: Nothing to worry about, that's for sure.

Guard 2: Nothing to worry about here.

Guard 3: Anything down the line?

Guard 4: Nothing. Up the line?

Guard 3: Quiet. These guys haven't got a thing here. I guess it's all quiet all over.

POEM

theirs
dug in the hangars
wag away like idiots at a bird
the broad ball rolling through a dream lake
quickens, feeling the wind, the breath, quicken
like a scarf caught by a gust
a cigaret
finds itself reading in a hand
making cutouts
from such real emotions
as love
as transcendence
somehow all look like smoke
the cares that have piled up pile-drive
into the skull of tomorrow
resting on the desk of today to accept neat ashes
zeros are at 4 o'clock
while 4 o'clocks bloom at five
at 12:05 pm, mayday, a lady leaves

YOU

you're looking forward
to something, and your faces
show it, *something!*
I stand over the smoke
entranced with your look
the beauty of your skin,
how much I love you
do I feel as much
if you were or when you
are ugly   a slight turn
to the right makes me wonder

IN THE MEANTIME

our letters
develop envelopes
to walk
to ride
to bounce
sightseeing
often off
human responses

it's asking

it's asking
too much to ask about
the view when the day,
one of days pulled
in the cold shoulder,
is putting edges on rooves
to look out is
interesting enough   to be
around is icing
so why say anything

SUNNYSIDE UP

My fine hand rubs across the knobs on the orange furniture
Each few nubs was like a little prayer bead worrying into the sky in
search of shape   Laffs oiled all the woods when a dream in ocher
walked in the crazy trapdoor at the back of my brain   The bronze
muted the harsh thoughts in the triplex where one traveled by light
from level to level

I was listening to the brown in my favorite elevator

A bois de rose commingled with a mist of vert bouteille that was
jewish in texture mediterranean in outlook and middle american
both before and after reason above rinsing like a cross between a
print dress and a snowsuit

Sit   Eat   Have some grapes   My toes grazing cement
and aqua from the decline of the chaise longue (adjust to desired
height)

The music was so wonderful I could feel it gritting my teeth rising
through my fingers to the back of my hand into wrist and OUCH
(shit!) banged my elbow   Right in the funny bone   That's
smart

This tan this is all a lot of hooey

Not long ago I ran into an old beau as a matter of fact my very first
beau on the street   And I was so shocked   His wife was so nice
And she smiled the whole time even when my old flame reached
right under my dress to see if it was the me I *guess* he remembered
He was really surprised that it was   And I was too   I thought

I'd forgotten all that   And we made plans to get together for dinner and a sail

He gave her that clean contemporary look that had little dick in large writing

And so The Bronzes have packed the car and left for two weeks for destination unknown

When we got up to the lake there was more swimming boating and barbecues than a soul could handle even with tongs   In two weeks this should last us till next year   By the second week I was thinking about work and home   And everything   I was raring to go

So we went with the orange   Rather leathery along the lifeline of the hand   The couch in its comfort is now stuck like a bone somewhere in the region of the shoulder   The lake was shaped like a lamb chop   From the sky the lake was shaped like a pork chop   From the woods we could make out the chop-chop of the lake   We were too late for dinner   It was over   It was over there   And we were over here under the skirt like a hand moist with memories

I remember once sitting around and waiting for Susy to come home with our first baby

Let me see   That was about two years after we graduated high school

I was sitting around with Carol waiting for Joe to come home
from his first job with Bobbie my first baby maybe in my third
month drinking some fresh-perked coffee   We were on our
fourth cup and we were really warming up to each other discussing
old times the kids the houses   And what we each with our
husbands wanted out of life   And everybody (it was such a nice
day)   And she being originally from California and me from
Ohio, originally   And I felt Bobbie kick me for the first time
I don't remember exactly the month

Well   It sure was tough going for those first couple of years
There I was with my first baby in our first house and Joe away all
day and I was alone with Bobbie until Carol came over and I knew
I had to make a good impression   I sure was uptight   We
were on our third or fourth cup of coffee and were really warming
up to each other   Talking about old times   The kids (we
only had Bobbie at the time)   Our houses   Carol turned to
me and said "Susan   I don't know if you know   But I think
we're sisters"   "Sister!," I said   And we hugged and kissed
and poured another cup of fresh coffee for each of us and talking
far into the night when the trains started to come in and we had to
each go home   But before that I took out the old family album
and we looked at pictures

A moist burst of sugar like shit on the tongue hurled me back in my
naugahyde reclining chair until my toes almost touched the ceiling
and my head the floor   I was at the console again feeling my feet
smell and my nose run   I was at a loss for words

I must have fallen asleep, I think

A breeze like two gentle hands brushed my eyes closed over a
mocha   I felt the couch seated in my heart as if in a dream

I was little   I was littler   I remember a voice   Yes, it was
my mother's voice saying to someone   "Look at that   He's
got the littlest dick I've ever seen   It's so cute"   And the
other person, I don't know if it's my father or not saying   "It's so
cute   Especially for a girl"

Just then an amazing bird flew in the window on a terrific gust of
wind and carried me up into the sky where all the clouds were as if
grown up

It was a party   And I remember   Coming in with my tutu to
kiss everybody good night   "Good night," they said

"Good night," the big bird says   And so saying I was dropping
into a chair for the reclining where I sat upon my metal arms staring
out the picture window waking up

The sky was a pale orange and the horizon like pillows on a couch
bore the weight of day no ill   My living body looked back like a
set of bedsprings making the heart with company hurtle through
time and space to another place   One that let with no coaxing or
coaching the fact sink in

A vision of modernity was scaling my peaks   And I could feel
the bronze vibrate with shimmers and the oils of woods sink
further in the grain and the grain opening under the laves of the
hand

A second hand was coming to rest next to the worrier   This in
search of handles   And when found these handles were pressed
as if by some powerful shorthand waiting to eventually with
addition of a little water be made into just the satisfying amount of
alphabet soup

And there we leave this feeling an eyelash on a cheek waiting to be
spotted and flicked off by some observer lover or other

A drain was clogging   I called Carol over to give me a hand
We drank three or four cups of coffee before we went to work
Joe was at work   I was at work when Susie's call flowed into my
brain   Something about a drain   So I just sent a sign back
And helped her   I think it was some hair

What a surprise to find a year's worth of hair   See you later
It's almost time for Bobbie to come home from school

Here comes Bobbie   Lunchbox in one hand schoolbag in
another skipping down the sidewalk with her little friend Bobbie,
but a boy even though their names are spelled the same way
They were avoiding some cracks in the sidewalk   And Bobbie
was making flowers out of hedge leaves putting them under
Bobbie's nose and popping them up into her nostrils as she bent
down to take a sniff   They both were laffing very hard and
walking very slow

Just then I got a message from Joe as to how to unclog the drain
at the same time Carol walked out of the bathroom carrying a
dripping minimat of hair to the garbage can

"Must be almost a year's worth of hair," Carol said   "Looks like
more than a year's hair," I said

She went home to cook dinner for her husband after washing her
hands   Bobbie and Bobbie were on the inside doing homework
They were very quiet   And that was nice   They weren't always
very quiet

I lit a cigaret   It was that time of day when everything kind of
stands still   Someone was whistling down the block   I could
feel that novel or movie I'd always dreamed about I had in me
come more to the surface   I picked up my needlepoint of three
roses and my mind and fingers worked on different wavelengths

A little girl is squatting in the dust of somewhere in the west   A
little pool of water gathers in the shadows of her dress that's hitched
up over her legs   Some riders come riding up to the house next
to the windmill in the distance   They hitch their horses to the
porch and walk into the house   The little girl stands up and skips
toward the house

"Would you like some water," says a weatherbeaten woman
standing near a tub   "Yes, m'am," says one of the riders   The
woman ladles out some water to a tin cup and each man takes a
drink

The little girl is standing in the doorway sucking her thumb
watching the men from under her hair   One of the men
turns to the doorway and then to the older woman   "Is
that your daughter, m'am," he asks   "Yes," says the woman
looking at a pile of laundry she's been ironing   "What's her
name"   "Bobbie"   "Hello, Bobbie," the man says to the little
girl   "Hello," Bobbie says around her thumb to the man
"How old are you, Bobbie," he asks   "Seven," Bobbie says
"What do you know about that," the man says, "Seven   Why,
Bobbie, I'll have you know, seven's my lucky number"

Better fix dinner

The sea air of Carol's voice uncoiled through the phone wire while
I was fixing dinner   I was telling her about these messages I get

from Joe that just seem to pop in my mind   Never mind, she said, have a cup of coffee   I get them too   I used to get them a lot more, she said, before I went to the spa and took those pounds and inches off my thighs hips and bust   I went there for a trial and have been going now six weeks and really feel great   I feel a whole lot better too   You ought to try the spa

I think I will   It's nice really to hear from Susy in the middle of the day but it kind of breaks into whatever I'm doing

Have a cup of coffee, they go away   Got to run   I got supper cooking   And I want it tonight to be just right   Got to watch those inches, Susy   Talk to you later

We are once again in the semiattached brain where the twentieth century is about to sit down to dinner this dinner radiating through contented rubbed bronzes is none other than the third square of three   The idea of the family is seated around the form of the diningroom table   The category of dishes are laden with an amazing array of flora and fauna   The wife, or feminine principle of this array, has forgotten the butter   She arises   Goes through the swinging door into the kitchen

Our refrigerator door swings open off its magnets with the gentle touch of the feminine principle's hand stroking the handle's chrome   The nine levels, or racks, contain an amazing array The feminine principle is *not* amazed   She is content   Her eyes search the racks for the butter while her hand finds it on one of the levels of the door   The door of philosophy shuts with a yum as she returns to the form of the diningroom table through the swinging door   And we leave, a little puzzled but most content, too

We can take this a step further   We could step into a lemon
yellow universe that smells so good   That we leave for today's
tomorrow whose nose is sniffing out the winds of change for
something to look forward to

I was looking *so* forward to going with you tonight Joe   We
haven't had a moment to ourself in weeks

I know, honey   But I'm tired   I was working hard all day
And now I just want to sit in front of the tube get stoned and go to
sleep   Is Bobbie still up   She's finishing her homework and
then I promised her an hour of t.v.

He's getting to be such a big kid   I wish he'd start getting a taste
for baseball   I haven't played it in years

Me either   Carol and me were fooling around the other day
playing catch with the kids   It's amazing how Bobbie throws just
like a boy

When you finish the dishes come in and watch some t.v. with me
Anything good on   Don't know

Well   We've certainly been able to fill a certain amount of time
there   A Monday's worth   Tomorrow's another day   And
so's the day after   The weather's changing and I think we're
going to have to dress accordingly

Yes, I feel so

THERE'S A MEANING

there's a meaning
in all this
but it seems
to have lost its address
first, let me
describe the house
that sits like a painting
in a cloud like a pudding
the day is behind
that's to say
the day's shaped like an ass
you spot
and decide to follow
it's so beautiful
for a second
I thought I felt
my eyes
moving along the jeans
along your thighs
until both of us remembered
somebody else
developed the term today
to cover
the period of light
that begins
with a start
and ends with a sentence
with a full stop
don't get me wrong
the fact

I've decided
to share my feelings
with you
has almost nothing
to do with you
you're my excuse
like a note from home
to trace out
what's bothering me
for all to see
but I'm making light again
earlier the beauties
of the flesh
embodying the day
were revealed
and even had enough
for seconds
a third reason
why I've decided
to send you this
is to issue you
a kiss
duly recorded
in the notebook of the soul
that's been thought of
for awhile
as some glorious hole
you shouldn't be too bothered
since neither you nor I
have the social sensibility

to expect problems from holes
this explains greatly
why we're like we are
today
on the street
grabbing ass

DANCE

breathing into the stencil
wakes up
the space that's (ah!) feet
a dream
of legs and knees
joined at the ears
goes into the mock-up
a willow frame
carries the evening
to the window
where it ignites
through the window
the window means something
else, but looked
like a look out
and turned out (ah!) like feet
to be where it should

DOWN THE DRAIN

Room just the right temperature
Birds singing in the cold day outside
Mind clear, body comfortable
Hardly the sense of any health
Turn over, in my mind, the rest of the day
Decisions drain on the table of consciousness
Listening to genetic radio codes
Through silver skull plate
Imagined to be terrific to have
In this second half of the 20th century
O bed
O chair
O cigaret
Unlit in my lips
Are flames awake yet licking
That make the prospect of the rest of life interesting
Do ask them to stay, please
And litter my ribcage with gravelly pleasure
As words on the ground
Bring to eye the mind of picnickers
Here I am in my thirty-first year
Bitching at everything
Trying to get ahead of myself in the line of light
And often like the wave in pompadour succeeding
Beyond my wildest dreams
O shower curtain
O windowglass
You were once in the picture
For the sake of air
Are now, backsie frontsie, in for the light

How I admire you
How I wish to make the same switch you make
As from light to shadow
As from red to pink to white rose
This consuming human fever is out to lunch
And I feel left spinning like a wheel on a spinning stool
O books, papers, pens
This arm that greets you with the moods
The move through adulthood
And winding paths through children
How the wish for machinelike precision
Moves fingers around your curves
And drips sweat into the curves of words
And makes light of the letters
Drying immediately when they arrive
When I'd be better off out for a drive
O imaginary car
With powerful engine
And hamburger bags in the glove compartment
Take me wherever I want to go
Before I know
Let me enjoy the sights
And see the seers and suckers
Blending into a beautiful american-made suit
Floating off the rack
Blown by a man-made zephyr
Into the arms of people, so beautiful,
Your eyes hurt
Before they close

SALAD DAYS

the sky is wearing a dress
and earrings and lipstick and
great shoes   and from where I look up
no panties   ONE MINUTE!
that's a great fake   underneath the dressing
a cock and balls is quivering
my god, it's pissing right down on the city
everybody runs for cover
the men in the men's room
and the ladies in the women's

CURTAIN

suddenly I was on my feet in applause   the cheers let go of my throat   I lifted to the ceiling with wings of my own larynx, and fluttered   a lazy feeling overtook me   I floated down onto the chairs

AFTER

talking
about
this
that
and
the
other
thing
neither
of
us
feel
any

GOING MY WAY

once
they
started
the
hills
were
rolling

HOW MANY YEARS IS IT NOW

How many years is it now
I've been living more or less
Out of a suitcase
Hanging around
Waiting for each poem
To put its nose out
And then, deliberately, GOTCHA
Multitudes of hamburgers
And hamburger multitudes
Have both done their multiples
Through my grinder blender
Where handwriting picks up
Where they often left off
And for meaning
A little catchup feeling
Spun out of desire
To keep up with my own sense
Have always been at least
Two years behind
Where mental and emotional
Development make me feel
Like an ass—the years pull
Away from the dock—who's
On a house call to the river

KISS

uptown a little something glitters
it is the brain of today
precise elastic a-hum
we are sitting in it smacking our weary lips
the lips smile
they seem to be on to something
they are afire, and yet watery

I open
my eyes

to let
you in

make yourself
at home

down in
a minute

SCALP EXCITEMENT

perpetual irritation sits like a pet
in the heart of america
fingers deft as sneakers
craft consciousness in traffic
the bureau of standards honks "hello, police"
in locales
depression enters the eye
watching   taking   thinking
and pumping up to the fantastic
it's breaking a hand
a hand in the making of a fist
moves like a movie through the land

HOW IS IT

I turn over
A new museum leaf
The light is new
And right on the spot
I was just thinking about
A fleet is about to set out
On the ocean light
Water turns to sky
And makes the eye
Blend ingredients in a bend
Shaped like an ear
A new speaker is speaking
I hear the words
They sound along
The halls of the balls
I turn to find them
As if I knew where to turn
Isn't that the sound
That's present
Isn't that the sound
That's gifted
Isn't that *something*
I'd like to put upon
The walls
And take down
Take apart
And put in a mood
The instructions to which
I say aloud

THE SANDWICH ISLANDS

The sound drives them wild   You can see them dancing toward
you somehow pinning you down   In your mind you mention
your mind and make the best use of them in your dreams you can
You put it to them   The sound drives them wild

The sound drives them to the store   Everywhere you look you
see signs of them   You note them in your notebook   They
begin to put themselves in the way of assembling for an oversight
overflight   You know them to be sincere   You see them every
other day   The sound drives them to the store

The sound conveys the message to them   You feel you know
them after an hour   You put them on the back burner of
your mind   You send them after some kind of imaginary goal
embodied in an imaginary body   You make them wait   You
float them over the bright water toward a bright future   The
sound conveys the message to them

The sound makes them wary   You also make them wary
Putting them first leaves you with regrets   Bob and Patty look
around and see them but pretend not to be startled   Bob sends
them a letter then shows it to you   Patty reads them a story and
allows you to listen in   The sound makes them wary

The sound looks them up in a book   Okay, you think, I'm going
to make them jealous   I'm going to make them green   I will
recognize them in one sitting if I'm very careful   You find them
between your favorite covers   The sound looks them up in a
book

The sound loops around them   You bring them a message from afar   Bob and Patty make them comfortable   They're only thinking of them   You make them comfortable too   You see them in a kind of recurring dream   You face them at face value The sound loops around them

The sound makes them go away   You can see them in the distance   You inspire them to write   Bob shows you a postcard from them   Patty makes them rub her back   Both of them make you a little nervous   The sound makes them go away

The sound makes them stop   You put them away for future reference   You put them off and feel how pissed off they are they can't help themselves   You take them for a ride   Bob and Patty meet them for dinner   The sound makes them stop

The sound takes them apart   Makes them so mad they turn a lovely blue   Making them wonder   Putting them down in a green book   Taking advantage of them   Making them take you along   Making them seek outside advice   The sound takes them apart

The sound butters them up   You float toward them in the dream I was just telling   You confuse them with members of the family   You tell them your life story   You bump into them every time you leave the house   You slip them the information and wait for a smile   The sound butters them up

The sound wires them in   You cage them with Bob and Patty be patient they'll crack   You put them into a pipeline of info and feed them to the computer complete with pix   You make them say what you want them to   You follow them around from pearl dawn to rose dusk   You project on them the colors of the current

surging through the ocean of your emotions   You limit them to a
few words   The sound wires them in

The sound deflects them   You feel them pulse as Bob and
Patty join you through the door   You seem to make them feel
comfortable don't be so sure   You confuse them with the
man in the hat   You make them pay strict attention to inhale
exhale   You file them under information for future reference
The sound deflects them

The sound creates them worrying   You fool them only that once
You call them on the hour   You feed them a line   The sound
creates them worrying

The sound curves them around   You take them with you
wherever you want to go to make them happy   You pull them
out of a hat   You summarize them   You make them into
a movie   Pull them over with you to a curb   Fill them
in   Carry them along   Stick your tongue out at them excuse
me I'm only fooling   You notice how beautiful is the sky coming
through them to you   The sound curves them around

The sound slips them up   You seem more surprised than
them   You feel them thumping   Bob falls to his knees and
thanks them profusely   Patty stands off to one side and makes
them place arms akimbo   You wait for them interminably   You
place them in a home   The sound slips them up

The sound nips them in the bud   Fun to write them press down
hard in blue   Fun putting them out of whack   Fun putting
them back together   Reuniting them with their families
You take them to a part of the country you've never seen before
You make them grow beards   You look them square in the

eye   You watch them move lips   The sound nips them in the
bud

The sound drives them home   You take them out of the car
You put them in a bag   You listen to them   You follow them
home   Bob and Patty are waiting for them   You keep them
at arm's distance   You make Bob and Patty take them in
Put them to sleep   Feed them a line   Prepare them for a
journey   The sound drives them home

The sound makes them ready   You sing them to sleep   You
wake them up   You call them   Bob and Patty who are often
wrong and not even there sometimes feel them coming to life
coming after them   You time them perfectly then strike   You
crawl toward them making them ill at ease   The sound makes
them ready

The sound completes them   You take them off the hook   You
hint hint to them they can take it   You flee them they follow
You take them apart they often come together by themselves
You have fun with them at no one's expense   The sound
completes them

The sound makes them wild   Bob and Patty put them away for
some other more propitious time   Bob and Patty put themselves
in their place   They feel them become a part of the unit   The
man in the hat carries them around in the eyes of his arms   You
can see them waiting a whole year for their turn   You can see
them fly apart at the wheel   You can talk to them through a gray
dotted mesh   You can make them listen but talk they'll never
talk   You can whiten and shorten them   The sound makes
them wild

The sound folds them neatly   You change them with the
other family members   You possess them sometimes dream of
possessing others put a smile upon your face   You make them
wipe that smile off your face   You see them through   You
follow them through the entrance to Bob and Patty's   You make
them take a neat white handkerchief for the pocket of silence
The sound folds them neatly

The sound breaks them   Looks them up   Refers to them
Puts them aside   Wheels them slowly   You talk to them in a
normal voice   You make them see things your way   Listen to
them   Sit them on a fence   Have sex with them even   Have
them even the odds   The sound breaks them

The sound puts them in a bag   You pat them okay that's enough
for now   You lick them against their former selves   Light them
from the inside   Take them from a great height   Free them
from themselves   They carry themselves beautifully   Free
them from any pain   You brown them up   The sound puts
them in a bag

The sound teases them   You call them from a great distance
Who told you to listen to them   You take them home and treat
their meat fever   Pull them over to the side   Ride with them
on the road   Feel them out   Research them then tell them
what's on your mind   The sound teases them

The sound fakes them   You imitate them and theirs   Bob
and Patty imitate them   You call them to you they come along
themselves   They themselves are conscious of an unearthly
but sound beauty   You play a part in how you see them   You
discover in them an amazing principle of organization   The
sound fakes them

The sound remembers them to you   You make them love you
deeply   You carve them in an old tree   You nourish them they
do the same to you   You cable them to a span   You feel them
creeping up   The sound remembers them to you

The sound fails them   You make them follow you and Bob
and Patty through the same out door   You feel them crash in
Callouses growing on them   Staking them to a claim   Stealing
them from a neighbor   You put them out to pasture in what
appears to them a school   The sound fails them

The sound makes them look up   Put them away   Fly around
them   Carry them over to the other side   Pin your hopes for
them on the in door   Booking them for later in season   The
sound makes them look up

The sound breaks them in little pieces   Hits them in their stride
Makes them put it away   Stands them on their head   Makes
them listen through walls nearly a block thick   Creeps around
them   Makes them pay attention to you   Carries them the five
The sound breaks them in little pieces

The sound underlines them   Patches them with dreams
Takes them for another ride   Keeps track of them   All of a
sudden makes them self-conscious blush rouge   Carries them
out   Freaks them out   Digs deep and finds them wanting
vegetables   Places them next to the water table   Keeps them
from ever entering   The sound underlines them

The sound covers them up   You can just make them out   You
can feel them all around you   You talk to them in such a low
voice   You can't fault them   You make them wait   Take
them aside   Call them finally   Let them in all at once   Let

them deplete all their resources   Refer them to Bob and Patty
The sound covers them up

The sound keeps them busy   They want to get in touch with
fingers with them   You exhaust them with all your resources
Rest them in a last resort   Pull them over to the side   You stab
them with your words in the heart make them feel enormously
badly   Cover them up with a shit-beige veil   Steel them for
future hardships   The sound keeps them busy

The sound gives them a new lease   You make them sign   You
hold the pen for them   You make them a life so complicated they
haven't got a moment to themselves   You look them up among
the greenish plants on Bob's and Patty's windowsill   Keep them
down not the you you know   You knock them around a little
Make them respond make them correspond with forces not under
their control   Make them fit   Take them for a break   Call
sweetly to them, how beautiful you are to me   Did you see them
when you were away   The sound gives them a new lease

The sound reaches them   Makes them take another way
Splits them almost in half   Carries them almost to sleep   Puts
them away for a rainy day   You complain to them to no avail so
what do you want them to do   You make them out   The sound
reaches them

The sound seems to obey them   You fool them but only for a
moment   You make a fool out of them   Meddle with them
Take them away from it all   Ask Bob and Patty to wait for them
but they don't show them the way   Feel them out their waiting
for rendezvous   The sound seems to obey them

The sound makes them crazy   You peel them back with your
shirt   You pull them apart   You make them into honorary
members of the family   Color them your favorite color   Take
them apart from that   The sound makes them crazy

The sound possesses them   You try to help them   You make
them say they're sorry   You combine them with a network of
other elements headquarters   You sit them down give them a
talking to hindquarters   Wild laughters make them seem kind of
calm   The sound possesses them

The sound gives them meaning   You lead them to a negotiated
understanding   You don't feel as good about them as you
once did   You make them late for the party with excessive
worrying   You take them for another ride   You forget them
they won't for a minute forget you   The sound gives them
meaning

The sound brings them up to snuff   Makes them want to kill
Sends them back where they came from piano and all   Hurts
them with the mother   Gives them a renewed understanding
between friends   Takes them out the teeth in the thick of the
thicket   Fires them with velvet envelopes   Covers them for
the local rag   Strips them quickly of their arms   The sound
brings them up to snuff

The sound makes them mind   You grow conscious of their
presence   You make them a present of your heart   Rip them
out your throat   You make them a part of your body wasting
little time   You grab them with grabbers at the waste   They
only will make themselves scarce   Look them in the eye   The
sound makes them mind

The sound exists for them only   You walk them through the out door   You fasten them to fascination   Keep them at bay staring at the estuary   Sleep between them the legs   Cave in to them and their demands   Lighting them with your lips   Pointing them out to others   Taking them into consideration   The sound exists for them only

The sound forgot them   You turn and look at them   Bob and Patty make them comfortable bring them something to eat Before them the day ends with them   After them a wallet speaks to the money talking turkey   You gobble them with other sustenance   You watch them go to the heart   The sound forgot them

The sound changes them at the window   You open yourself to them   You cream them   Take them apart put them back get together with again   Keep them from leaving   Do them in Take them off the case   Allow them to follow their ownership lights   The sound changes them at the window

The sound understands them   Gets them to fend for themselves Fills them up with food and coffee   Returns them to their point of orange   Detaches them from me   Claims that that's not them   Puts them to work   Fields any questions for them Screens them and then proceeds to see you to them as if that was necessary   The sound understands them

The sound goes away with them   You talk them into the dream you were just having where you talk them into going to the movies having a bite after then to bed to fuck then sleep them off   You make them exchange electrons take in orphans   You rush them into something they didn't want to go into   The window opens to them   The sound goes away with them

The sound lets them keep their clothes   Paragraphs them in
a strange feathery language   Puts them in the same room as
the man in the hat   Goes toward them in forward   Fleeting
glimpses of them   Craves them and their lives and times
Interviews them for the papers   Puts them on easy does it street
Seems to understand them   Strips them of their ease   The
sound lets them keep their clothes

The sound surprises them   Makes them comfortable among
themselves   Concentrates on them   Feels Bob and Patty
should have left them alone they're too often too much anyway
Too little for them to make a difference   Exactly what it is to
them   Exhausting them and then sorting   The sound surprises
them

The sound recognizes them from their pictures   You picture
them   You make them take away any distinguishing features
You invite them over to look them over   Follow them to the ends
of the earth your mind's dog-ear has been turned to a dogleg
Submit them to city scrutiny   The sound recognizes them from
their pictures

The sound finds them in the central chamber   You take them
off your hat   You will them into your life   You make them
believe in you   You tell them where to get off and watch them
listen   You carry them to Bob and Patty's filling them in   You
repeat the necessary info is all to them then let them out on their
own   You watch them enjoy themselves   You point some
chances out to them   Stuff them in a car   Carry them beyond
the point of no return where it's funny   Create through them a
defense of the region   You make them a house   The sound
finds them in the central chamber

The sound clambers for them   You take them the money
They let you get close to them   You find them strange so what
doesn't everybody   You theorize to them through the blueness
guitar   You disgust them with your strums   The sound
clambers for them

The sound cools them   Resets them among the others
Resigns them to their face   Whispers to them sweet nothings
Takes them for granite   Poses to them a portrait insurmountable
international problem   Turns them down on their application
Fills them with silver crayon loathing tipping the equilibrium the
other way   The sound cools them

The sound puts them in your place   You want to take them
seriously but do you   Listen to them when you're listening to
yourself   Make them feel at home   Take them with you when
you go   Bounce them off one another   Make them do what
you want them to do   Record how you feel about them   Make
them into a small book with wing covers   The sound puts them
in your place

The sound curls them around your little finger   I'd love them
to think you weren't here   Look out and after them while I'm
gone   You're not known to them   They often mistake you for
one of themselves   You often need them to tell you what to do
The day shines on them among others   Otherwise you won't
when you see them recognize them   The sound curls them
around your little finger

The sound funs them   You have set them at dim   You free
them from their leaps and bounds   You take them for a fool
You put them in your place but fail to understand what's going on
with them   To you and them everything seems awfully glass

You can hear them freezing in their tracks   You assume them to be size places   You exhaust them when you talk so loud   The sound funs them

The sound costs them   A whole lot of things make them think A whole lot of things are going on to them   Visualize them from what you know   You don't think you'll be able to disappoint them with what you were wondering about them   Repeat them once in a while   Look in on them   The sound costs them

The sound comes to them all at once   They recognize Bob and Patty in them   You forget to take them with you why don't you Compare them with what you know   Put a little color in them Occasionally show them and yourself a good time off   Burn them with your desire   Flames cut in to your numbers   The sound comes to them all at once

The sound keeps track of them   They want you to join them in enjoying themselves   Make arrangements for them   You'll know them when you come across   Spirit them toward the apple of the impossible   Don't mention them to anybody   The sound keeps track of them

The sound makes them work   You know them is to love them You keep them next week to your heart   You space them out You watch them grow   You make them lose their way along with themselves   You undertake to discover them wherever you find them   The sound makes them work

air
joins
us
in
song
in
places

MUFTI EXPLODES

Mufti explodes
Inside the sunglasses
Windows draw upon the city
A clear view
From the other side of the river
Glazes the sun
From the inside the car
Conversation describes
What a day at the beach
The streets are almost empty
And flat with people
At the other side of the tunnel
Traffic's pouring into a cup
Glasses become washers

DELICATE PETALS

Delicate petals
Tell me *how*
They enjoy
My smooth skin
Changing temperature
As my hand
Changes leaves
I wish them
Well, well
I trust them
They dictate a
View to me
Launching flesh

EVERYTHING SEEMS

A faint uneasiness
A shortness of breath
Each little thing wrong I suspect
Of being more than it seems
And so it grows
To be more than it seems
There are no specific examples
Everything falls into
What I've been saying
These are my words

OVER THE EDGE

Over the edge
Sparkles supply
A large part of the light
Required to lighten
The mood
          Chimes
Are in the traffic
Going home
Those are the lucky ones
The ones going home
The unlucky ones
Never left the home
             Driving
Is just one of the many
Ways of leaving
And expressing

HOW WATCHFUL OF PASSERSBY

How watchful of passersby
Is great eye in the arm
Brushing daily with death
The leg upon the teeth

Pretty pretty water
Went into the door
And sought the neighbor
Through the floor

Passersby are entering
The doors with exit signs
The eye on arm is blinking
Back a tear and sigh

EYELIDS TURN

Eyelids turn
In darker grease
On green jade sleeve
Off arms
On back of chair
Light through slat blinds
Lets in
Slightly used air
Let out the nose
Slightly used air
Making foyer to
Lungs stucco
Opening all-purpose room
In slightly used air
In brain's showroom
Foil
In a turning ball
Sends light
In spokes that speaks

ALMOST AMAZEMENT

Twice floating inward
Slow of pace
Where a meeting of the mind
Is mere mental activity
Minded work
Asking   Asking
Watery ceiling
Let mind drift off
In beautiful handwriting
This is for me   Don't do me any
So by lengthening
Thin angstroms stunning
Develop a nature frowning
Lawn green
You're too tense
Throat continuing clearing
Remark way voice breaks in half
Dismembered and thrown into fantasy
Rejoicing in fragments

A TECHNICAL REPORT

We'd like to thank everybody in general   They've helped to make
everything possible   They have brought us fields and streams
The fantastic droop of a summer afternoon   The wonderful
feeling of highways and byways   The transistors in our machines
that help us over the bumps that stress stresses and eases us into the
easy life

While everything is not now available to everyone it should and
soon will be   The divided self no longer will be   But will rest
come to rest in one place at one time to allow one person's being to
flower   All the days of his or her life

You know that hideous feeling that defies description   One of a
whole family of such feelings   That will go the way of the horse
out to pasture with the herd   It will only be used for pleasure
For example   When one of those feelings comes upon us it will
be as if we were in a very important thrilling steeplechase with a lot
of riders riding   The excitement would be breathtaking

Everyone would have pretty much what was needed for a happy
life without attendant worry   Babies could have as much apple
juice as they could drink   Children could have anything they
wanted within reason   Adolescents would have dates anytime
they so desired and also could have anything they wanted   And
they could stay in or leave school as they wish whenever and would
find school if they decided to stay there interesting tailored to the
needs of each individual *as an individual*

Young men and women would find no trouble getting training or
schooling for any job they were interested in doing   And when

they were finished learning the fundamentals they would not have
the slightest difficulty finding work   Work would be fun not work
in the traditional sense   And money would be of little interest or
no interest on the choice of what work to choose

A variety of family structures would be available *and normal* so that
those with no children or not raising kids would find a place where
the necessities and niceties of life would not be a burden to the
individual but would become part of the household whatever that
was

The old would not be discarded as just worn-out members of
society to be shunted aside and forgotten left to die alone   They
would be able to make contributions in the form of wisdom drawn
from experience since they wouldn't have to worry about physical
well-being which would be provided   They could prepare
themselves for the road of death whichever chosen

You know of course that everything will be very easy to get done
Basically what is needed is nothing more than a little common
sense   The kind of sense we sense underneath what appears to
be insolubly complex   It is much like Louis Agassiz telling his
students to keep observing fish day after day after day   The fish at
the end contains everything there is and everything you wanted to
know   And with some patience everyone is able to make out the
common sense simplicity that is the complex fish

It is very important—indeed it cannot be emphasized too much
how important it is—that everyone must act in such and such a
way that his or her self-interest directly correspond to the interest
of everyone else   A small step for mankind might take place if
everyone at the same time decided either to set his or her watch *to*
that time or at that time to think of everyone else in the world
Another possibility might be to have everyone in the world say

the word *love* at the same time   These should work and leave
everyone once again with the spirit that motivated the founding
fathers and mothers to have kept everyone in mind when they
founded every country in the world

We find that race creed and country of national origin play no part
in the vast makeup of the world as we see it   Everything harks
back to the little things in life   The sound of running water in the
country   The sound of a brook in the city   A faucet filling a
kettle with water to make coffee and tea because some friends just
stopped by   The laughter of little kids

These are just a couple of timeworn things that evoke pleasure from
a frothy genesis   There are others and will be others   Before
we go we should try to think of some more so when we come across
anything everything won't so much surprise us as issue forth like a
fountain gushing with delight at the mere presence of the beat of
life

OPEN THE WINDOW TO THE SOUL

A band

On forehead
Soaks up notes
And sits damp
Over the work

Ions

Work overtime
And get time and a half
On the job

Pursuant

To feelings
The day before
Covers the mind
With sensational glitter

Pulse

Works its way
Out along the fingers
Where a song's coming
Out of the orange rose
In the bluish rug

Fire

Lights under the griddle
Raises glasses
And toasts toes
With nectar from the neck

One eye

Shuts up finally
Like a mouth
And sleeps behind the other
Where a couch

Interprets reasonableness
Through slipcover consciousness
                              Woe
's on the ball
And perfumes the foyer
With a conversation between
Spiritual lawyers
Laying down the law
                        Far and wide
Like ayes and nays
Landscape stays home
                          Tongue
Peels and crushes same
Like a combination hand-foot
And eats same
Like an all-purpose organism
The third generation this is
                          Listen
Carefully and learn
Something of use
                      Enthusiasm
Is only the patio
Behind the organism
Where smoke's hardly
Visible in bright sun

AEOLIAN HARP

Air blows in window
Over five o'clock shadow
Of first spring day
Thoughts and feelings
Spring and harp
Radio accompanies me
Perfectly like a circle
Pick up phone
Talk to a friend
What's new   What did you do
Took a walk crosstown
Took a walk in mist last night
Reminded me
Of one of your poems
Reminds me night's coming soon
Company's coming for dinner
Different persons
Line of symbolic meaning
Leap in and out of the stream
Of consciousness   Take a break
Turn off attention
Something's been nagging me
Last couple weeks
Spring coming on?   Today, relief?
Standing at door of change
Turning knob
In its own little circle of friendship
Kin to hand
Electrons travel through
Fingers   Little hearts

Move through heat of blood
Lines moving together through
The visual form something
Recognizable   Been meaning
To tell you for the longest time
I appreciate what you've
Recognized in me   How we're
Similar the same different
The shadow's passed now
To the chin of the sky
Taking on it the sunset

FORM-FITTING HIPS

Form-fitting hips
Wait for the snow
Lips wait
For the mouth to activate
And say something nice
Drift over each
Letting know
The perfuming through vowels
Prepositions like birds
Fly in the face of reason
And prepare dinner
In an inner face
The cooking fires are lighted
And lights go on
Around the city
A twinkling shirt
Slips over the sky
Like an enormous adjective
Sweater filled with sparkle
The tall buildings
Look down and inward
Contemplating their corridors
While the other buildings
Breathe through doors
And talk
Window to window

clouds hang in the distance up
bird-wheels for pushpins
leading like threaded reds to point-houses
windows light from within and reflect out
imagine occupants for pains   the heart within
beats a little faster as the clouds
falling from the dropping sun drop in (a purple-red)
a hunger for dark just making itself
felt in a hunger for dinner   lights
go on one by one making no dent in the twilight
the clouds get lost in the sky
as the sun gets lost in new jersey
beige and green-blue lights drop halos
on the passers underneath on varying streets
the mind sleeps in the thinner footsteps
the heart slows
the body sleeps in the greater new york area
as parts of the moon go up

THE EVENT

all
great
minds
think
it
likely

ART

the
final
break
with
the
past
is
made

birdsong
kick
this
single
happy gesture
thru
the backbone
of America

SEATED ON A HILL

woods
with
sky-rags
come
through
the
leaves

AS IF NOTHING HAPPENS

As if nothing happens
There's a flower
And we've been there
We're among its petals
But, without thinking,
There's another flower
And we're there too
The sudden colors,
They're a kind of love
While the feelings
Are late at night,
Very nightlike, awful
In their nightness
And we find ourself
Sleeping alone sleeping
Alone, too far along
We're tangled in traffic
We return elsewhere
But our thoughts
There's a flower
It's another
They are with us
We're lost for words

OH, MY GOODNESS

Oh, my goodness
Where'd I put my wig
I can't be seen without it
I'd rather go out without a car
There
Get off my wig
You're not even supposed to be in the house
Who let you in
Where's my shoes

WHEN LOOKING OVER THE ROOM

When looking over the room
Heart leaps into chairs
Isn't that amazing
Letting the heart do something
Like that   The body
Used to be Joan across the room
Isn't there, just covers
Folded back waiting for sleeper
To return   Wonder if door said
"Thank you, call again" as
She left   I wasn't here, so
I can't be faithful witness,
Believe me I'd fess up right
Smart, push my coonskin cap
To the back of the argument
          Remember when
Winter used to come in the cold
Weather, that's all changed
Now I am captured by age
And must wear their chains
Pronoun and noun don't agree
Squeamish glances directed at
THE DOOR   Capitals portend
But don't work, just sit around
Heaven all day, that's the ticket
               By now
Joan should be uptown hard
At work, probably thinking of
Good reasons not to get home
Early   Maybe if I do this long

Enough, that bum Ted will get
Another job, let me off the hook,
That what you want, Joan,
After all these years of moving
Right along to move right along
I sense a serious note   The bird
Throws its voice out of the tree
The tree throws itself into the view
As if there's no tomorrow, which
There isn't, what a nice phrase
                Which there isn't
It's got a ring, meaning that's
My guy, or gal, whomever   The
Tea's almost ready to cross take
Out the bag, and eyes dot from
Lack of sleep tossing and turning
Worrying worrying worrying
What am I worrying about
Isn't there always more worry
Where that came from   Lean
Back, Ted, light a cigaret, and
Drink deeply from the soap

THE DAY FOLLOWING

Impassioned short sections of window, she said, would be nice to
accept when it occurred to her (at the sound of her own voice) one
of the words none can define, happiness, or its corollary keenly
alert danced with painted a masterpiece of intimacy in the middle
of the room past friendly and sympathetic like every sensible man,
looked as though through her legs who year in and year out (turning
the light on and off) opened the door to the set of the street
Even this is not enough: at home   On the contrary, while the
water hums and boils who will doubt what is going on in front of
their nose, the building of a house   A new surface a new film of
dreams would be poured in with the foundation   Heaps of abuse
will be flattened to make a yard contained by a cyclone fence
Perhaps needing a clip, a patio will make itself felt in the back of
the house—next to the green cellar door—arabesques cut into the
surface of the cement by a one-legged skater with a cane

It is this osmosis of contrariness that lifts the spirit very much in the
same way a heel does a shoe, ever so slightly and hardly noticeable
It's on this particular membrane the drama of frailties carries its
latent despair to the point of nationality

Now, this is all very vague   Would the same earring that takes
so much pleasure in jangling find equal success in terms of the
regionalism of the ear   Would the ear, in *its* turn, be willing to
submerge the interests of the mother country, the personality, to
the interests of the constituent parts, the body the brain, the ins
and outs of their existence   Would the intimacy descend upon
people like a new leaf

Who knows   (Who will ever understand the relevancy of those
hands just thrown up on the stage from an otherwise perceptive and
appreciative audience)   Who wants to know

An interpreter was sent for to help with the seemingly tangled
language   "The most important thing to remember, thought," he
said, "was that the mirage and its denominators, while flexing the
ego, have thoroughly prepared themselves unconsciously, to let fly
at only—and *only* at—short-term importances, and those only
Those points only, to get a cup of coffee, cigarets, three squares, are
not negotiable   Whereas, if the cards are played right you'll find
yourself with a long hand and happy face"

"Let me give you a little example," he continued, "suppose, just
suppose that you want three countries . . . no, it doesn't really
matter which three . . . your hip pocket   Well, it won't do to be
hasty   Be patient   And most of all, *be* alert   The slightest
thing, the raising of a tiny joint of the finger could be the dead
giveaway that you're right on track   So you know, *now*, that you
must build your pipelines in the direction of that particular rep
He will most probably give you the specs by nightfall if you're
willing to exercise patience and caution"

"On the other hand, *you* can let *him* know by some subtle
intelligent gesture that *must* leave the general demeanor of the
negotiating team intact   You can ask, how the wife (or wives
if he comes from a polygamous part of the world) and kids are,
how's the new house, is his mother feeling much better, his new
car is wonderful you have the very same year model yourself, and
betwixt all of this be sure to nest your gesture, a quick wink perhaps,

repeated, maybe, so there can be no doubt, but as natural as a very pretty ear on the beautiful head of a dazzling and enchanting woman"

"Please don't forget what I have told you   If you forget, I'm sure that your interest and attention will decline, over time"

OUT OF THIN AIR

The wind is picking up
A lover   A person
Hollers at the buildings
Sitting here, I've sat here
Many years
Listening and watching
A window buzzes and
Sizzles gossiping with
Night   I don't know
If this makes sense   It
Moves me over

WHEN YOU START

When you start
to miss somebody
and it's not
the somebody you miss,
nothing's missing
something else is happening,
what that something else is
that's for someone else to say
Nuages begin to be nuances
which is interesting
and attention gets attenuated,
often there's traffic
but in another sense
there's a possibility
so much is stress
making a body feel klunky   Look
at yourself this way,
when square's passed
through a cubism
even Plato might have drooled at,
doesn't sex
in an infinite nostalgia
remind you of something's somebody,
terminating in competition, you
win you lose, that's the way
it goes, the real you, when

POEM

clouds
over
the mountains
are like
clouds
over the mountains

industrial
amazement
turns
to
      slush

THE OUTLYING DISTRICT

From that height the city looked like a circuit   I was downtown,
and by plugging myself into a particular reflective source of energy I
was able to make some progress   All music at a given time made
itself available to the viewer   And, although everything appeared
as peace and as one, those who paid strict attention were able to see
signs, this was not so   But to go back to the beginning

I got home from work the same time as usual   After unlocking
the first door entering the tile hall I tiptoed over the mail, bent and
sorted it for which apartment   I dropped the others' outside each
door and went up to my place

I hadn't bothered to clean up after myself last night   The pan,
still with some chicken and grease in it with a light orange barbecue
sauce sat on the two left burners of the stove   The dirty copper
kettle, half-filled with water, was on the right front   I turned on
the flame under it and made myself some coffee

It was a Thursday night, and I could feel myself looking through
Friday forward to the weekend   I stepped back, looked at all
the shit in the sink, thought about nothing much for a moment,
rolled up my sleeves washed the dishes   Something nagging and
hanging wash was on my mind   While you were out of town

Two sugars and milk were in the coffee   I opened the afternoon
paper and on the fifth page turned my mind to afternoon   Here I
was and am with nothing to do writing to you about it   I haven't
got the slightest idea what you can say in return   This is the hard
put part of the day to get through

Weather changed to atmosphere and that to mood   Brushes
of irritation moved slowly up and down my spine counting the
number of knuckles in the backbone   Lightning flung itself more
than a foot from the body through fingertips not expecting so much
to be going on in the after-lunch world

There was a switch on the wall   I walked over to it and pushed
"On" while I thought of a famous person whose name I forget
right this minute   Things poured down golden ladders fixed
to platinum beams into each of my cells   I felt giant and tiny
by turns filled to the top of my skull from the tip of my feet with
alternating public and private feelings   Known and unknown
voices jumped rope in my ears and met the prepared for this brain
halfway

I decided to go out   Turned left on the sidewalk walked down
to the avenue   Shops were filled with records books foods
beverages browsers and shoppers   The curious and the curious-
looking   A man and a woman walked through one shop that was
half sidewalk in a film   I was almost startled by how relaxed
A whole family—three generations—drove up to the curve in a
battered car, tumbled out and went every which way, leaving the
car ajar

A ten-year-old something-or-other came up to me and said, "Hey,
Mister, Mister! Why can't you never starve at the beach?"   "I
don't know," I said, "why can't you never starve at the beach?"
"Because of the sandwiches there"   I gave the kid a slap in the
back of the head, just enough to make his ears ring

I walked along   Soon found myself in a strange neighborhood
I'd walked through here once or twice, but the details I didn't know
I went into a luncheonette and had a cup of coffee   While I

drank I watched the clock and felt the tip of the clock watch me
Something I couldn't quite put my finger on was getting writ large
in back of my mind   I was possessed by crowds and felt myself
become a valise in the collective mind   A redcap picked me up,
put me on a handtruck and pushed me down the ramp to Track 13
(one of my lucky numbers) to wait to load on the train

There was an observation car, from which I could watch the sea
to shining sea as the train passed leaving whistles in the ear of the
gorgeous dumb blonde countryside as we passed   Such beautiful
thighs!   My whole mind at that second didn't mind turning
woman, but soon it said "Hungry," and it was back for a complete
sumptuous meal in the dining car watching towns and villages go
past, as if we—the baggage—were standing still and the landscape
was on the move

My companions at dinner were a mother, father, and daughter
The two females were proper but the father—whew! (here I wipe
my brow!)—was I glad when that meal was over   After nodding
hello, etc, the first thing he says is "Woman walks into a shoe store,
sits down in a chair and puts her foot up on the stool to wait to be
waited on   The salesman sits down, and looks up asking 'What
thighs!?'"   Big laugh   Meaning, more where that came from,
pal   The females addressed me as "Professor" the rest of the
meal

The coffee finished I continued my walk north (or uptown) passing
banks stores and museums hardly a person every now and then
on the street   The sun was making the air warm and I got a lazy
feeling   I sat down in a park with a waterfall and watched the
waterfall up into the, following my own eye, apartments above
Living, I knew, in one of these apartments was a fading great beauty
who spent hours on chin alone

No one had seen this person for years although every six months or so the papers would run a story in the subjunctive about who *was* who in the good old days and this person played a prominent part The wrist of real society   The one to whom it may concern, the world was a bauble to be swallowed endlessly on outstretched tongue   And endlessly swallowed   Not out of lick-lip nervousness, but of delight   The last known public picture had been taken more than twenty years ago

Clouds overhead were getting to be more and more substantial paragraphs   The mind's eye followed them into buildings, alongside reflections, and through a deep blue filled with the music of the delta   I could hear the sound of a tractor away behind the tree and the river underneath all that   I looked at my shoes   I held my hand out palm down and looked at my nails

When I got outside I turned right   There were small houses, people in cars, mysterious low but wideflung buildings with guardhouses and peepholes in doors that might have been mistaken for a main entrance   I walked past several of these and felt my curiosity being aroused

I knocked at one of these warehouses   The peephole opened up and a voice kind of squeezed past the eyeball out   "Who are you?   And what do you want?"   I gave the voice my name and said how my curiosity had been aroused, the peephole closed, and I stood facing the door long enough until it finally dawned on me the door wasn't going to open, and I went away on my way

Many years later, after an explosion the mystery of this particular building was revealed   This was nothing but a building with a guard built around thin air   Some person was using the building to save the space from other usage   But that had receded so far

back in time, and the guard was paid automatically by mail—there'd
been several generations of guards—that whoever remembered
what was going on forgot already

In this direction the streets were much littler, as if they came from
a small town, and gave off the aura of ministering to the spirit   I
can't tell you how happy I was to get out and get a little fresh air
I was starting to go a little nuts in my own two rooms—as much as I
loved dearly those rooms, and the sunbeams that beat their heads
against the putty walls

This way I stopped for a soda and contemplated the straw   My
mind rushed back to an earlier time when I was growing up, and
worked at a fountain in a candy store   I looked at my wrist and
realized I'd forgotten my watch   Then I realized I never wore
watches anymore   I figure if it's important enough for me to
know what time I can always find a clock   This attitude has
worked and played well with me for many years   But once in a
blue moon I forget and revert

As I sip my soda through a straw one eye goes out the heart of the
window watching passersby   Cars and trucks join people in
my own panorama   A street comes into the avenue right at the
mailbox in a tee and I get the long view down to the next avenue of
escape

I started out filling in candies and sodas every day after school
Also, filling the syrups and cleaning all the stainless steel spigots
and fixtures along the fountain   The job was to take a barely
damp towel and shine everything as if buffing a shoe whistling
all the while like in the movies where the whole station moves
in time to the shoeshine boy   I got a good idea this way what
was popular   I always had to fill in chocolate and some vanilla,

rarely cherry or coffee   Ginger ale, club soda were always down,
pineapple rarely so   Chocolate bars and gums always needed
filling

I'd finished the filling part one day and was doing the polishing
when a middle-aged whitehaired man sat down right in front
of the spigot I was working on, shining so much I could see my
reflection   I heard a voice say, "Have pride, Kid!," and looked
up to find the voice went with the whitehaired man   I kept on
buffing   "Psst   Have pride!"

Now, the spigots were past shining   I was confused   So . . . not
knowing who this person was and wanting to find out before saying
something totally insulting I went over to the boss and told him
what was going on   He laughed and said, "Oh, that's Paddy
The Rabbi   He's just giving you the needle"   I went back
and finished the job listening to Paddy's admonition every two
minutes   Over the next few years there we became fast friends
But we've since lost contact

About a year later I was allowed to make sodas for the customers
after spending a lot of time practicing on myself   The key soda
at this particular fountain, the soda upon which every other soda
based itself, pretty much, was (and still is) the egg cream   This
had to be made *just right*

Depending on the size glass, the large one the most frequent
made, two fingers of cold milk fill in seltzer to where the white
bubbles just go over the rim of the glass, let settle into a firm white
top, *slowly* add a couple of fingers of syrup from the bottom and
carefully, *carefully, now!*, stir up from the bottom slowly the whole
concoction so (in the case of chocolate or "regular") you have
a cloudlike white head on a chocolate body   Carefully add
enough soda water to fill glass to the top   Remove spoon without

bruising the milk and *serve* keeping fingers away from the top of
the glass   Be sure to collect the money about the same time a
customer empties a glass

If the Rabbi was in the region he'd usually be sitting giving
advice by the minute most of which was funny and he knew was
ridiculous, but he expected the difference to be learned fast

The pride advice *was not* intended to be funny   It was only later
through hearing stories of Paddy on the cops that the full import of
"pride" was filled in   Oddly enough, it contained an elaborate
sense of the privacy of human tragedy   For instance, Paddy was
coming down in an elevator off a job with his partner and a nosey
elderly woman on the elevator kept asking what happened

Paddy said, "You know Mrs. Jones who lives on the 15th floor?"
Yes, the lady nodded   "Well," said Paddy, feeling the hook take,
"well, she was living with this gypsy who cut her head off with a
broken hacksaw blade"   The door opened and the lady puked
Paddy was the first person in the first person who I ever heard say,
defending me or something I said to other men his age, the old days
weren't so good   They were all that was there, that's all

My steps were shorter   My lingerings over details more detailed
While my walk to the left included shops etc, to the right parks and
gardens, sunsets, the interiors of panoramas held my attention
It's still too early to go home

Even now I'm a sucker for advice   I'm always willing to let
someone tell their story even if I know what's what, and know no
surprises in store   I get to meet some very strange people that
way   One just the other day caught my attention by mistaking
me for a famous Hollywood actor, Cary Grant, I have to admit,
where in the confusion and me denying I was Cary Grant I gave

the man a quarter for a cup of coffee that used to cost a dime
Several hours later I had to unconfuse myself   I mused crossing
the intersection and started to get a glimpse of the true depths of
the organization of the earthly city

Electrons fired through the red parts of the nervous system until
below the knees activated at stroll and went   The whole world
seemed a *smaller* more manageable place to live in, living in the
world   I had to take a leak, took the stairs two at a time, and
was home *voila!* prepared to spend the evening in cooking dinner,
doing a little reading, maybe watch some tube

I washed the dishes   Straightened out the livingroom, put the tan
pillows on the couch back in place, straightened the rug with the
gardens in it surrounded by burgundy, poured myself a beer, lit a
joint, made a cup of coffee, mixed a drink, brewed a pot of tea, cut
a morsel of meat, filled a pipe with opium, turned on the television,
picked a record I wanted to hear, changed my clothes and opened
one of several books I was reading at the time

The sky outside and the one I was thinking about turned, with
envy?, I don't know, a horrible green   My mind was sucked
between the covers and obliterated the voice of the narrator that
bounced from crag to crag in a sunset of incomparable written roses
Noses began to bleed spontaneously and verbs went out of toes
A voice in the backyard—I got up to look out—said to a wandering
cat, "Hey, what are you doing?   You'll ruin my garden"   The
cat kept going

I learned to like particularly the color of the cast of thought I was
thinking   Different years out of the past accompanied different
years in the present, to provide a ground of memory upon which
to pattern existence   One minute like a leaf   One minute a
leaflike pattern blending into general petalness

Rising and sinking, like hope, is the only way I'll describe my
experiences   To say that evening provided a resume is to speak
too soon   In mid-paragraph, remembering the mail I'd forgotten
to read, I went to my desk, sat down and sorted through   I won't
waste your time telling you what kind of shit was there I didn't want
to read   I put each of the pieces in some order of interest—which
was and is low—cut open envelopes, read tore and threw away

Something it'd taken years to prepare me for was in the making
If you look behind you some night on a quiet almost deserted
street you'll have some idea how I felt   The velvet of my feelings
provided a canvas upon which I felt a horse glowing with the wan
eyes of a child   I embraced and was embraced in turn by that
light creature   My hands were knobs and my mind the machine
they tuned   I was grounded in philosophical principles and
antennaed with the rabbit-ears space and time   My thoughts on
either I won't even waste your time with

I left the book on the green table bent backward on its spine   I'd
understand some nights to remember   My heart was . . . how
shall I say it . . . my heart was in a glove   It was the glove itself
It was the love in glove itself   It was the hand on the behind
behind love   For a fraction of a second I knew I'd cracked the
knuckle on the thumb of the hand of the riddle of the universe
Just as the joint cracked, a voice said "You can't guess?"   That's
all I remember

Weather thoughts other turned over tumbling dry in the past like
an inventory   Time to turn and turn off the music   Time to put
pressure on the retina   Time to let me see you more often after
hours of traveling   A calming effect on the whole metabolism
and circulatory system   A reexamination of the foot, or pedestal,
of the body politic, removal of callouses trim nails remove the
ingrown toenail of the heart   A narrowing of expectations

But what happens?   I no sooner narrow my expectations, renew
friendship with old friend, then I realize the sense of abundance
that was felt surging through the economy before the scandals—the
level—would never be reached again, too expensive, in anybody
here's lifetime   This gave pause to the horse   Why waste time
overworking when overworking doesn't do one bit of good   My
mind swam the breaststroke with the above realization

But below, it was business as usual   Each skin on each
instrument and piece of equipment was wiped entirely clean to
avoid irritating the works   Just enough was left undone to jog the
memory tomorrow what you can do today   Hearing is largely
impaired and you can't see your hand in front of your nose

That doesn't mean we didn't love each other deeply, but
what's that on a scale of one to ten when a living is what we're
talking   From one of the deepest wells of the brain the thought
"Look both ways before crossing" welled to tears in my eyes

FROM THERE

The wish blew
Across what I read
Of course, the breeze
Is what I meant
But so much easier
It is to say something
Else and take it
From there
Yell below
And start to go
Refusing to (to) wait
For you, why you
Always late, why
I always early?
The sunset, so it goes,
Is orange
As if a shears
Had pinked trees

HEARTSTRINGS

in case a call came for him
he went down quietly
while he was shaving
while she watched him
the siren docked nearby
selling a picture of friends
a bottle of white wine flourished
conscious of being ridiculous
of course not help gazing tenderly
the summer kept you waiting
a glimmer of a smile welled
for example, why roam
the man with a total grudge
do you understand why
clapped a hand on your mouth
pacing the witnesses to interview
missed by a hair
her young thoughts with a hesitant air
bowled over by existence, this island
echoes suited them they stayed
filled with smoke to start on
standard in front an old-fashioned design
rosy complexion huge lips disappointment
a shirt sleeve but not least
riding days india
otherwise pleasure scents
ironical
twinkle
eye
gardens from the sea

voice husky, took notes
a motion
a place
a circumstance
tentative nerves blabbed about about
blue and white stripes the other way

TALK'S DISAPPEARING

Talk's disappearing
Into a cloud
Reappearing periodically
In the window
Direct view of the sky
Provides a magazine
To the waiting room
Of the eye
The eye talks to the hand
Above the water tower

ATTENTION

he happened to touch her hand

it was a strange thrill

how many had reveled in her beauty

in beauty, generally

in the vast pleasure house of people

TO HOLD

To hold
Everything you need
On each
Wonderful day
Saving
Time and money
And information
Inside tips
When to find
Stores open
Up-to-the-minute services
And one-per-family
Vouchers
To enhance
Your stay wherever
With each one
Who has been chosen
Name where
You *will* stay
And (snap)
There you are
In heart of heart's
Of a city
In a country setting
Near the shore
Brilliant with
High international
Standard light
King- and queen-size beds
Cocktail lounges and bars

Coffee shops
Swimming pools
Night clubs
Dinner and classical dancing
Saunas
And shopping arcades
All add up to *refrigerator*
Snack bars
Spectacular views
Health and beauty spas
Complex overlooking lake
Private terraces
Same-day laundries
All add up to *radio and taped music*
You arrive in time for a swim
Visit
The home
Of the greatest art in the world
Arriving in time for lunch
And latch on to
Cloud-high remarkable beauty
You want
And do
Write home about
All adds up to *wander on your own*
Cities as serene as a river
Surrounded
With yourself
With a quietness so intense
Even footsteps and heartbeats seem to echo with

All calling your name
All adds up to *a constant fragrance*
Lazy pleasure gardens
Cruise and drive through city after city
Cool, along with breezes, your face
You visit
Between free day and free night
You've dreamed
A short walk
Not far from your place
Don't know
Exactly where
A border
Leads into a plaza
Somehow supported
In midair
By angels and demons
During free time
You are one of each
Even though
(That's the breeze you hear)
Neither lasts long
Traffic streaks
Along tantalizing aromas
Lights flash
Workers rush by
Watches and wigs in
A shimmering blue and gold glow
Explode 50 feet in the air
You are
The last person
To enter the dark corners
And complete
With your 2 feet

Planted firmly on *terra firma*
An alphabet
Cool off
On warm afternoon
And relax
Unwind
Soak up magic
That surrounds you
And may well be
Well worth
Time and effort
Life centers
Around the beauty and
Remoteness, the
Beauty and re
Moteness, you've
Been seeking
In so many ways
In so many
Here is an island
Between then and now
All adds up to *off the track*
Unchanged during
Remaining almost

SPARE HOURS

today, at noon, S T and D demonstrate at City Hall for superior
foods   they will be met, on or in, at the nearby park by the
inseparable friends C P and E   from there, they will move
uptown, and will be met later, on the way, by X and B

when they got to City Hall S T and D found that they were the
only ones there   no one else had shown up   where were C P
and E, they thought, and what will happen if we don't meet X and
B as we planned   will they wait for us or leave without us, you
know

well, S T and D decided to go get some lunch and come back later
they were probably early, they thought, since no one had shown
up yet   and if that was the case, no reason to worry yet about
meeting X and B on time

in the luncheonette they each ordered meals: S had a cheeseburger
with onion and a coffee malted; T had a plate of chow mein with
rice and a lemon coke; D, who wasn't very hungry, and had a cold,
had a toasted english and tea with lemon

just as their meals were put in front of them a friend of D's, Alice,
walked in the door   they said hello, shook hands, and talked
back and forth for a few minutes catching up on each other's life
since they last saw each other

D introduced Alice, who was called by old and close friends, Bob,
to S and T, who in turn were known to their old and close friends
as Kit and Paul   since Bob was a friend of D, who had no other

name, although sometimes answered to the name Jack, Kit and
Paul were treated as old and close friends of Bob's

when they got outside again, and walked to the park, S T D and
Alice found that thousands of people had gathered under the
weeping willow trees carrying banners and posters, drinking hot
cups of coffee, drifting from group to group, saying hello to old
friends, tying bandanas of all the colors of the rainbow around
their necks (to be used as masks in case of teargas attack), checking
helmets, and generally doing the same so they wouldn't be
separated by the march   S T D and Bob did very much the same
as the others but had promised to be back in 15 minutes and meet,
under the old oak tree that, as a *gris eminence*, stood out like a sore
thumb among the willows

suddenly there was a helicopter   it swooped out of the little
narrow streets and went round and round swooping just above the
treetops

later, S T D and Alice met under the oak   they were joined by L,
who had gone to school with T, and who had shared many political
demonstration experiences with T   to his old and close friends
he was known as *er* because of his manner of speaking

in a manner of speaking, the crowd started to move uptown
groups of people drifted into the streets and dribbled into the
avenue that would lead them most directly to their destination
uptown, the superior food convention

after they had walked about an hour, S T D Bob and *er* decided
to go get a cup of coffee and warm up   they trotted into a
luncheonette and ordered   the other people in the luncheonette
tried to ignore them, but they, S T D Alice and L, knew that
their every word, look, and gesture was being hung onto and
being weighed and tabulated pro or con   suddenly there was a
helicopter

after they finished their coffee, and warmed up, they went outside
and joined the stragglers on the march   by walking fast they were
soon able to make up the distance between the stragglers and the
main drift of the march

as if by chance the five friends bumped into a group of people who
were sort of zigzagging from curb to curb chanting O - O - O O -
O, when they came upon C P and E locked arm in arm with the
group   the eight friends hugged kissed and jumped around in the
air   everyone got to know everyone else   suddenly there was a
helicopter in the air

when the eight friends got uptown they were met by X and B
the ten friends hugged kissed and did little dances around each
other letting everyone get to know everyone else   suddenly they
thought they heard a helicopter in the air but, no, it was a city bus
loaded down with passengers peeping out to see what was going on
the ten friends waved hello to the people on the bus   a couple of
standees waved back

much later, the demonstration broke up and the ten friends went
off, milling down the street, to go and have a party, some wine
food and grass in Bob's apartment   on the way downtown they
stopped in an all-nite deli and bought some goodies

they leaped walked and tumbled up the seven flights of steps to
Alice's apartment   they opened the door and deployed through
the room   Bob took out some chilled wine, C P and E unpacked
the food and sweets from the deli, X and B took out some papers
to roll the good grass that S T and D had just bought, and brought
along, into joints

later in the evening everyone was having a good time   only scraps
of food were in the plates, cigaret butts and roaches overflowed the
ashtray and everyone was warm and comfortable

Alice's livingroom was like a park on the day spring comes out
the ten friends talked and hummed and let their limbs overlap
suddenly there was a helicopter in the air

someone was at the door they thought, although it sure sounded a
lot like a helicopter   do you think we should let them in, or just
ignore them   suddenly they thought about a helicopter   it was
in the air

BAGGED WHIMS EXCITE

Bagged whims excite
The assembled   They come
Apart and assume
A feather lightness and
Fly up, crisp and suddenly
As if struck by flame
The line moves at a constant
Pace with the bedazzled order
Of art   Hubcaps go on
The knees with a rap
Out-of-order knuckles are
Rapped to go and weighed
With a ruler   The assembly
Appears white and neat

LOCK UP THE CHAIRS

there'll be
no more sitting
around   no more
movement in
circles   no more
this and that
we'll lock the door
close and seal
the windows and
button our lips
no word will we
utter   no sound
will we make
no more will we
be thought
more dead than alive
we'll solve
each problem that
plagues us and
causes us to turn
urgent   and causes us
to affect sleep
forever not to be

TED GREENWALD was born in Brooklyn, raised in Queens, and has always lived in New York City. He is the author of over thirty books, including *Licorice Chronicles* (The Kulchur Foundation, 1979), *Word of Mouth* (Sun & Moon Press, 1986), *Jumping the Line* (Roof Books, 1999), *In Your Dreams* (BlazeVOX [books], 2008), *3* (Cuneiform Press, 2008), *Clearview/LIE* (United Artists, 2011), *Own Church* (Spuyten Duyvil, 2016), and *Common Sense* (L Publications, 1978; Wesleyan University Press, 2016). An online reader's companion is available at tedgreenwald .site.wesleyan.edu.

MILES CHAMPION was born in Nottingham, England, and lives in New York City. He is the author of *How to Laugh* (Adventures in Poetry, 2014) and coauthor, with Trevor Winkfield, of *How I Became a Painter* (Pressed Wafer, 2014), among other books.